Brands We Know

Ford

By Sara Green

Bellwether Media • Minneapolis, MN

Jump into the cockpit and take flight with Pilot books. Your journey will take you on high-energy adventures as you learn about all that is wild, weird, fascinating, and fun!

This edition first published in 2017 by Bellwether Media, Inc.

Library of Congress Cataloging-in-Publication Data

Names: Green, Sara, 1964- author. | Green, Sara, 1964-
Brands We Know. Title: Ford / by Sara Green.
Other titles: Pilot (Bellwether Media)
Description: Minneapolis, MN : Bellwether Media, Inc., [2017] | Series:
  Pilot: Brands We Know | Includes bibliographical
references and index. | Audience: ages 7-13. | Audience: grades 3-7.
Identifiers: LCCN 2016004390 | ISBN 9781626174085 (hardcover :
alk. paper)
Subjects: LCSH: Ford Motor Company--History--Juvenile literature.
| Ford, Henry, 1863-1947--Juvenile literature. | Ford automobile--
History--Juvenile literature.
Classification: LCC HD9710.U54 F673 2017 | DDC 338.7/6292220973--
dc23 LC record available at https://lccn.loc.gov/2016004390

Printed in the United States of America, North Mankato, MN.

Table of Contents

What Is Ford?..**4**

Henry Ford...**6**

Growth and Change..............................**10**

Ford Classics **12**

Ford Today..**14**

A Drive to Help.......................................**18**

Ford Timeline...**20**

Glossary **22**

To Learn More **23**

Index...**24**

What Is Ford?

The fans cheer as drivers climb into sleek cars. It is almost time for the NASCAR race to begin. Several drivers are racing Ford cars. These are among the fastest cars on the track! The green flag goes up and the drivers are off. All the cars are speedy, but only one can win the race. The checkered flag is waving. The race is over. A Ford crossed the finish line first!

The Ford Motor Company is an American automaker. The company headquarters is in Dearborn, Michigan. Ford also has locations in many countries around the world. Ford makes sedans, trucks, and sport utility vehicles (SUVs). It also owns another automobile brand called Lincoln. Ford is one of the largest automakers in the world. People across the globe recognize its blue oval logo. It is one of the most famous automobile brands on Earth.

By the Numbers

nearly
$150 billion
in sales in 2015

more than
15 million
Model Ts sold over time

over
$1.5 billion
donated from the Ford
Fund over time

201,000
employees in 2016

30,000
Ford employees
volunteering each year

worth
$54.2 billion
in 2016

Ford Headquarters

5

Henry Ford

Henry Ford founded Ford Motor Company. He was born July 30, 1863, in Dearborn, Michigan. His family lived on a farm. At a young age, Henry often took apart toys and watches to see how they worked.

Henry left the farm and moved to Detroit in 1879 when he was 16 years old. He worked as an apprentice at a few machine shops. There, Henry learned about an internal combustion engine that was powered by gas. At the time, steam engines often burned coal. Henry was curious about the different machine, but he decided to focus on steam engines. He found a job working with steam engines in his hometown, Dearborn. When his father gave him some farmland, Henry started a lumber business using steam power to saw logs. During this time, he met his wife, Clara Bryant.

Henry Ford   **Thomas Edison**

A Famous Friend

The inventor Thomas Edison inspired Henry Ford to build an internal combustion engine. The two became lifelong friends and enjoyed camping together.

Henry Ford

In 1891, Henry and Clara moved back to Detroit where he got a job at Edison Illuminating Company. Henry also wanted to make his own internal combustion engine. He worked on the engine in his workshop for several years. Then in 1896, he attached it to an open carriage he called a Quadricycle. It had one seat, four bicycle wheels, and an engine in the back. Henry had built his first automobile!

Quadricycle

1903 Model A

Henry was determined to improve his design. He experimented with delivery wagons and racecars. Soon, other people believed in Henry's dreams. They gave him money to start his own automobile company. In 1903, Henry started the Ford Motor Company. Henry and his team built the Model A. The first one sold for $850 and could go 30 miles (48 kilometers) per hour. Within a year, the company had sold more than 1,000 cars!

Growth and Change

Ford rolled out the Model T in 1908. The Model T was cheaper and higher quality than most other cars at the time. Henry used an assembly line to produce the car. This made the process quicker and cheaper. The Model T sold for nearly 20 years!

In 1919, Henry's son, Edsel Ford, became president of the company. He helped introduce a new Model A in 1927. This was the first new car from Ford since the Model T. In the 1920s and 1930s, Edsel also led the development of the luxury Lincoln line and the mid-priced Mercury cars.

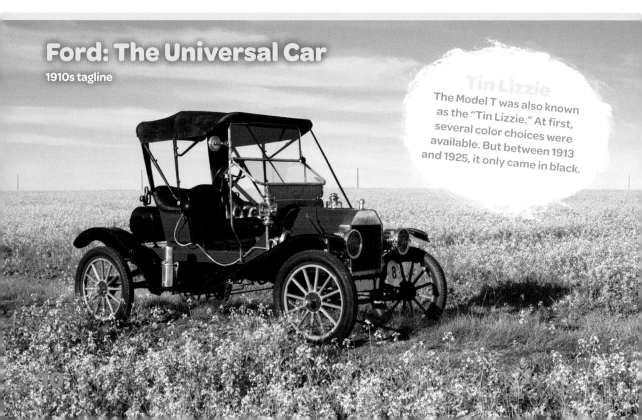

Ford: The Universal Car
1910s tagline

Tin Lizzie
The Model T was also known as the "Tin Lizzie." At first, several color choices were available. But between 1913 and 1925, it only came in black.

Henry Ford II   Henry Ford   Edsel Ford

Ford was in trouble by the 1940s. Sales were low, and employees were not happy with working conditions. Edsel's son, Henry II, helped the company come back to life. He became Ford's president in 1945. Soon after, he hired new managers. He also made Ford known overseas. In time, Henry II and his team helped Ford become one of the largest companies in the world.

Ford Classics

Over time, Ford has designed and built many classic cars. The Thunderbird, which was introduced in 1954, was one of its most popular models. The first model was a convertible with two doors and two seats. It was created for both comfort and power. The line continued until 2005.

The Mustang came out in 1964. At first, it only came as a coupe or convertible. In a few months, Ford introduced a model with a sloping roofline. It was called the fastback. People loved the car's sporty look. In 1966, Ford sold more than 607,000 Mustangs. That was the most Mustangs ever sold during a single year!

Seventh heaven on wheels
1950s Thunderbird tagline

1955 Thunderbird

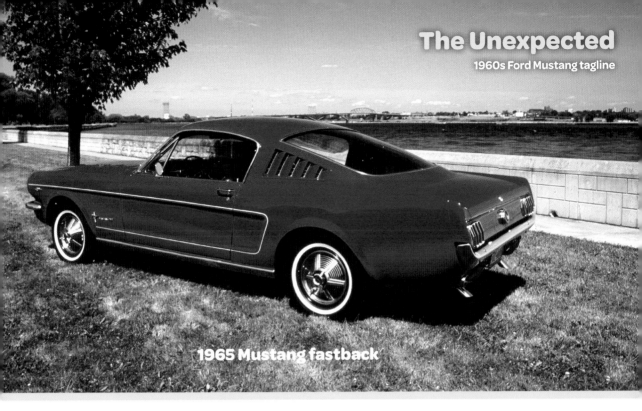

1965 Mustang fastback

In 1968, Ford rolled out a muscle car called the Torino GT. It was known for its speed. In time, Ford added a more powerful engine to the Torino that made the car even faster. The car was renamed Gran Torino. Torino muscle cars were popular NASCAR racecars. They cruised racetracks until production stopped in 1976.

A Ford Flop

Ford introduced a car called the Edsel in 1957. Many people thought it was unattractive and too expensive. It also used a lot of fuel. With low sales, Ford ended the line about three years later.

Ford Today

Today, millions of people around the world drive Ford vehicles. Since 1948, Ford has sold the popular F-series pickup trucks. They are powerful and built for hard work. Over time, the trucks have become smoother and more comfortable. Ford F-150 pickup trucks are among the top-selling vehicles in the United States!

Ford also makes popular SUVs. The Escape and Explorer are sturdy, comfortable, and fun to drive. Ford sedans, such as the Fiesta and Focus, are also top sellers. A version of the Taurus is often used as a police car. The latest Ford GT thrills sports car fans. Its power makes it a top racecar!

Built Ford Tough
1970s-2010s tagline

Popular Ford Models

Model	Main Body Type	Year Introduced
Model T	runabout, town car, touring car	1908
1928 Model A	roadster, sedan	1927
F-1	truck	1948
Thunderbird	convertible, coupe, hardtop	1954
GT40	coupe, racecar	1964
Mustang	convertible, coupe, fastback, hatchback	1964
Torino	hardtop, sedan, station wagon, fastback	1968
Fiesta	sedan, hatchback	1975
Taurus	sedan, station wagon	1985
Explorer	SUV	1990
Focus	sedan, station wagon, hatchback	1998
Escape	SUV	2000
Fusion	sedan	2005
Flex	SUV	2007

Taurus to the Rescue

Ford introduced the Taurus in 1985 to compete with Japanese car makers. It later became the best-selling car in the United States from 1992 to 1996!

GT

Fiesta

Escape

Ford also produces cars that run on electricity. Some are all electric. Others are hybrids that use both gas and electricity. Models include the Focus and Fusion. Fuel costs are lower for hybrids than for cars that run only on gasoline. They also produce less emissions. This helps keep the air clean.

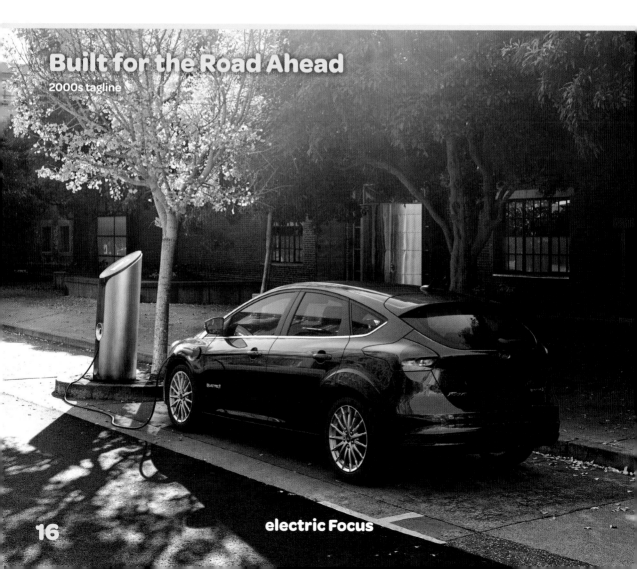

Built for the Road Ahead
2000s tagline

electric Focus

driverless car

Ford vehicles come with a variety of options. Ford offers a system that alerts drivers when other cars enter the side where they cannot be seen. Another system helps drivers stay in one lane. A self-parking feature is available for some models. Cars can find parking spaces and pull into them without help from drivers!

Today, Ford is also testing driverless cars. The cars map their surroundings and plan routes. They can detect cars, pedestrians, trees, and other objects. The cars steer themselves and follow speed limits!

A Drive to Help

In 1936, Edsel Ford started the Ford Foundation with $25,000. It grew to become one of the wealthiest charitable organizations in the world. It supports projects that help the poor and improve equal rights for people all over the globe.

Another way the company gives back is through the Ford Fund. Henry Ford II started the fund in 1949. The Ford Fund has given more than $1.5 billion to communities around the world since then.

Many Ford employees serve as volunteers. They build houses, plant gardens, and provide food to hungry people. Some volunteers work on water conservation and collection projects in countries such as the Philippines and Argentina. Many dig wells and lay pipelines. Ford is not only a leader in the automobile industry but also in serving others.

Darren Walker, Ford Foundation President

Ford Timeline

1863
Henry Ford is born in
Dearborn, Michigan

1903
The Ford Motor Company
is founded

1913
The first assembly
line is started

1919
Edsel Ford becomes
president of Ford

1896
Henry builds his
first automobile,
the Quadricycle

1908
Ford introduces
the Model T

1936
The Ford Foundation
is founded

1945
Henry Ford II becomes
president of Ford

1996
Ford rolls out its first
electric vehicle, the Ranger

1947
Henry Ford dies
at age 83

2016
Ford wins the NASCAR
"Driving Business Award"
for the third time

1949
The Ford Fund is
created

2010
The Ford Fusion wins
the Motor Trend Car of
the Year award

1966
A Ford GT40 wins its first
of four Le Mans races in
a row

Glossary

apprentice—a person who works for a more skilled person in order to learn a trade

assembly line—an arrangement of workers or machines where work passes from one to the next until a product is put together

brand—a category of products all made by the same company

charitable—helping others in need

classic—popular for a long time due to excellence

conservation—the protection of animals, plants, and natural resources

convertible—a car with a roof that can fold back or come off

coupe—a car with a fixed roof and two doors

emissions—dangerous fumes

foundation—an institution that provides funds to charitable organizations

founded—created a company

headquarters—a company's main office

hybrids—cars that can use both gas and electricity for power

industry—businesses that provide a certain product or service

internal combustion engine—an engine that burns fuel on the inside

logo—a symbol or design that identifies a brand or product

luxury—very comfortable and expensive

muscle car—a sports car with two doors and a powerful engine

pedestrians—people who travel on foot

sedans—cars with two or four doors and a top that usually cannot be removed; sedans seat four or more people.

volunteers—people who do something for others without expecting money in return

To Learn More

AT THE LIBRARY

Bullard, Lisa. *Ford Mustang*. Mankato, Minn.: Capstone Press, 2008.

Maurer, Tracy. *Ford Thunderbird*. Vero Beach, Fla.: Rourke Pub., 2008.

Venezia, Mike. *Henry Ford: Big Wheel in the Auto Industry*. New York, N.Y.: Children's Press, 2009.

ON THE WEB

Learning more about Ford
is as easy as 1, 2, 3.

1. Go to www.factsurfer.com.

2. Enter "Ford" into the search box.

3. Click the "Surf" button and you
   will see a list of related web sites.

With factsurfer.com, finding more information
is just a click away.

Index

assembly line, 10

brand, 4, 10

Bryant, Clara, 6, 8

by the numbers, 5

charity, 5, 18

classic cars, 12, 13, 15

Dearborn, Michigan, 4, 6

Detroit, Michigan, 6, 8

driverless cars, 17

Edison, Thomas, 6

electric cars, 16

Ford, Edsel, 10, 11, 18

Ford Foundation, 18

Ford Fund, 5, 18

Ford, Henry, 6, 7, 8, 9, 10, 11

Ford, Henry, II, 11, 18

history, 6, 8, 9, 10, 11, 12, 13, 14, 15, 18

hybrids, 16

innovations, 8, 10, 12, 17

internal combustion engine, 6, 8

Lincoln, 4, 10

logo, 4

Mercury, 10

Model T, 5, 10, 15

NASCAR, 4, 13

Quadricycle, 8

sales, 5, 9, 10, 11, 12, 13, 14, 15

sedans, 4, 13, 14, 15, 16

sport utility vehicles, 4, 14, 15

taglines, 10, 12, 13, 14, 16, 17, 19

timeline, 20-21

trucks, 4, 14, 15

worth, 5